THE
TRUSTY SERVANT

THE
TRUSTY SERVANT

Andrew Jordan

Shearsman Books

First published in the United Kingdom in 2022 by
Shearsman Books Ltd
PO Box 4239
Swindon
SN3 9FN

Shearsman Books Ltd Registered Office
30–31 St. James Place, Mangotsfield, Bristol BS16 9JB
(this address not for correspondence)

www.shearsman.com

ISBN 978-1-84861-844-2

ACKNOWLEDGEMENTS
A Festschrift for Tony Frazer (online), *The Fortnightly Review* (online),
In the Name of the Voice, Ostragehege (Germany), *PN Review, Shearsman, Wild Court* (online).

The author is grateful to The Winchester Bindery, 11 College Street, Winchester,
for use of their print of The Trusty Servant.

Canst thou draw out leviathan with an hook? or his tongue with a cord *which* thou lettest down?

Canst thou put an hook into his nose? or bore his jaw through with a thorn?

Will he make many supplications unto thee? will he speak soft *words* unto thee?

Will he make a covenant with thee? wilt thou take him for a servant for ever?

Job 41: 1-4

CONTENTS

THE SEA

Identifying with a force that no-one then could articulate,
I concealed myself amongst mysterious coercive things;
a slab of sombre fish, the cracked quartz of bloody ice
and slit belly of what lay cold. A rubbery, dissociated head.
Dazzled at the door, I paused and then, as always,
checked for reactions and cues that might imply rewards.

Now everyone agrees that beauty overlies an unknown power.
We all accede to love's ambivalence. And yet there was a time
when ideals, fully realised, did not imply regrets. Inscrutable sea,
I found my compromise in the love conditional, its dark and
fathomless complexities, commands and signs, and thus
immersed in it from early on, grew gills and fins and spines.

ORFEO

Swaz hie gat umbe,
daz sint alle megede,
die wellent an man
'alle' disen sumer gan.

Giving up the ghost, I went alone to the ford where the dead,
still in open rebellion then, stood before God's vengefulness.
He, in the form of Philip, Landgrave of Hesse, commanded
mercenaries as at Frankenhausen in 1525. But now a chorus
heralds *Fortuna*, who turns her wheel and moves the Moon,
at its full, across the Sun, eclipsing Splendour. *Pro Fortuna*,
accepting fate, I took my chances behind her wagon and saw
a hand lift the shroud for a lady to look upon that mustering.

Half-lit vapours rise at sunset from a creek. Follow this line
with your eye and you will come to the silhouette of one
making haste far off on the marsh. Dusk fog obscures
what happens next. When they can, men will look for him.
On Friday evenings at the pictures, with my friends,
I saw objects cast in beams from way back, symbols
transcending my first understanding, but not my corpse,
marching amongst carrion, beckoning from the screen.

Looking over my head, one lady holds up a flower labelled *Ioye*
and the dead, cheering, pledge their loyalty to her playfulness.
Through lustres dolorous, hidden forces animate decaying flesh,
and there I am, phosphorescent, on screen, with a maiden
I admired before she died. Spectral, in living memory,
she smiles. Desire ignites regret. Quickened by the thought
of lust, almost touching but not intimate, passion flagellates
and this is why, wanting more, those who passed still agitate.

Reliquias receptas. Through these songs, recovered from antiquity,
I also was drawn to consider what once I would not have,
that rights deny tradition, leaving those long gone forlorn.
Unselfconscious love, childish or innocent, informs the one
who rises when there is no other option, lifeless and cold,
from the effigy of everything we have forgotten, or denied;
the dead possess and move freely through that body perilous,
its constitution, within which all hopes and liberties are bound.

In Walsingham the pilgrims gathered in the pub to celebrate
their victory. Our ancient dead at rest beyond the wall. The jollity
of pretty girls in drink. Catching sight of himself in a glass,
the little priest lifted onto the bar by some great beast sees Death
behind him as the spirit lights his face. He's ready then to confess
that his was transcendent bliss, that he enjoyed nothing
but a harmless kiss; and he sees them all as they'll be judged
in the dark outside the inn when only the idea of love lives on.

On the Quay, outside the Fleece, fishermen watched as he,
in jest, held his child over water which, far below, echoed
their laughter. Cassiopeia, archaic Queen, head pushed back
amongst stars, I also was helpless. But now, looking up,
contemplating the night sky, seeing gods and monsters,
each caught in its moment of apotheosis or regret,
abstracted, emptied, lit and horrified by what it sees below,
I long to make myself at home where once I felt degraded.

As I sat reading quaint old English verse, a hair, tickling my hand,
moved me to inspect the place where, much like a bookmark,
it was caught. Thus the trap was primed. I saw it there.
To know what justified this low device, I ventured in
and lost myself amongst the leaves. Turning
amidst *Honters with hornes* and hounds, the hind, desolate,
fell as *thai halowyd hi hi* full joyful, whilst 'drery Dethe',
drawn by its cries, unmoved by what he saw, looked down on me.

An unknown ship, silencing Sirens, crossing the bar, navigates
the run and, riding the tide, enters the harbour where, turning,
it bumps the quayside. On board, men speak a strange tongue,
their words weighing what we have left unfathomed.
Castor, Heracles, Iphiclus, son of Thestius, Peleus and Jason,
Orpheus; they disembark and head straight for the Fleece.
What had the sea perfected in those men who went,
heroic, half brute, into that grove, dark beneath its emblem?

No warrior, nor valiant king, can equal Orpheus, Calliope's boy,
son of Oeagros; from early on he featured self-erasement in a song
and undid orgiastic gods to come. And this was when men
and gods went dancing with animals. *I liked that frenzy.*
Silent mouthpiece, oracular powers might infuse a grove
but I cannot see my way past Sirens, drowning them out.
Disembodied, gagged, inside my head is a listening voice
and it's this unlikely epic singing that now floats mythic Argo.

Bacchantes, extempore and thus liberated, ran out of chaos
and I stand where they danced to mete a form of stability;
their ironies, although long depleted, can still turn a word
upon which we rely. Moved to the scale of fantasy,
bounding horizons celestial, they'd go crazy. In that state
I also attack the image with bare hands: kaput, the head
sees a torso, limbless, thrown and now we too are hands,
knees, teeth, feet, the eye within dissolving completely.

Orpheus, illustrious laureate, please note that although Hades,
once implacable, wept, it is not your song he wants, but its loss.
This is the self-erasing image: erotic force cannot be grasped
and a poem in its passing is exquisite. *You are not what you were.*
Since entities that wielded power—formulations, bodies,
states and their elites—resigning past glories, took down
their own symbolic array, defacing what had been vital,
your stopped mouth, heroic, adds pathos to our regal silence.

As those recently butchered grin and gape on the ground,
horsemen tarry along the bank of a deep double ditch. Black,
with dusky gleam, tired beasts muzzle steam. In frozen snow
they stamp this image: across the moat, brilliant in moonlight,
the tower shines "as if cut from paper". Yet to be undone,
time hurries to a fast hand. These armoured men,
at a signal, advance toward the bridge that, lowered,
appears to welcome them to sanctuary or stronghold.

Death's men stood on either side whilst she, unsteady on her feet,
could not be the object of the quest, nor yield to it; imploring
better than the rest, I cheated Death with how I sang. Really,
he's not impressed but Persephone is and, carried away
by her wilfulness, he gives in, sits back, eventually, gets pissed.
I left them telling stories in the hall and walked from the palace
through archaic roots of rhyme with her, breathless at my back,
stressed, limping iambic, her footfall measured, keeping time.

With her not far behind, I pushed through the press of dead
who, arriving, holding weapons, rehearsed the funeral march.
In Nether Hades, fording a stream, turned once only
for that look-alike phantasm. 1974. On the Buttlands.
Grainy and indistinct. *Carnival Queen with Attendants.*
Her loss reverberates through my physique. Heurodis,
what leapt from your heart when, waking, you saw Death,
keeper of tradition, ruddy in gold, before whom I paled?

In summer heat to honour Mab, the fairy queen, the Royal Hunt
with sundry beasts rising and falling—and there they are, turning
in the blur—a lacquered horse, a cheerful dad, imago antelope
and golden car where Brenda, bound within that dress, now lurid
under lights, with painted lips, accelerates the image with her passing.
Pearls or berries where the woodwork is so adorned.
On the edge of an abyss she waits for no shepherd. The tangent
nerve from this nulled form voids the shadow on the marshes.

Although trees, beasts and birds, moved by him, gyrating
in spirals and rows, have long-since perished, leaving no trace,
stones persist, alone or in circles, to mark their fall.
I catch glimpses of dancers, spinning damp tresses,
skirts flaring at his command; fast unfurling nymphs,
transformed; youths, horned and hooved, screaming
as they see what he becomes—man and god, hunter and prey,
bone doll, blood-fiend—as in their midst he tears himself apart.

And then the grandeur of Death's standard bearer, some risen
half-rotted thing; framed by the breach, victorious, he indicates
that I also must follow. Sitting with my parents near the back,
I saw in cigarette smoke curling through the beam
elongated figures yet to reach the screen.
Lit by their lustre, shades of those I had lost
and everyone I knew, and people I had yet to meet,
thrown into the splendour of the blaze above the seats.

Seeking respite from Phoebus' rays
I sat on a gloomy bench
with Edward Young's *Complaint*
in my lap (Lorenzo, such a boy!)
as time would pass that way.

I called for a voice and sang for a song
and staggered for a dance upon
the clefted hill, Parnassus' top,
Bevis Mt. etc. as Pope would have it
from the pages of some antique book.

And then these glades among,
trim and stylish in appearance,
Belinda, sportive play'd, and Eloisa
sighed in yon sequestered shade.

Each plays the essence of its kind
to impart a pleasant sense of the other.
Precise and absolute, this Beauty cast
in peril now of ravishment, still shines.

THE TRUSTY SERVANT

The bores hede, I understond,
Is chef service in all this londe,
Whersoever it may be fonde,
  Servitur cum sinapio.

I was made in a butcher's shop where these were on offer:
fatty loins, meaty chops, bristling flank and your pale breast;
brawn jelly; pork cheese; a tasty bit of tongue.
Offal bin scrapings. My people are recovered meat.
In bodies disparate, ill-made, we manage these utilities:
a serviceable if imperfect integrity; efficiencies both
economical and moral that you might profit by; thrift.

I note that you have found much in me to admire
viz. seen in the flesh, a form fit for a rollicking caper;
an open countenance; a chaste tongue speaking volumes
allegorical upon fleshy essences of porker, ass and stag.
Just as every species is separated by a figure, so am I
the singular, all-in-one, product of a sum. In addition,
each instance of my image, once seen, is multiplied.

Surveying the prospect, you thrilled before my potency.
Now, neither seer nor seen, transformed into a principle,
I become your gaze. Proud mutant. Bound instrument.
Private utility. I carry piety like a master wears his coat;
that is, with belly and loins protruding. I pushed my snout
into your trough and now you suffer those differences
imagined in the time when male and female were sexes.

Invoking beasts, you unleashed this figure of a man
that now, discerning dangers, you'd keep separate.
Laughing when you laughed, I grew coarse;
careful not to offend, I planned little gifts that might limit
my greed; this, so that you, finding me wanting, might want more.
Casting off my clothes, I climbed upon your back
and you, grunting and squealing, pretended subjugation.

At work amongst gentlemen I pass my master's table:
"Next time with bull's horns, auroch-shouldered, he'll labour
with Europa on his back." Beasting me, they bray and bark,
but I recall her hands gripping flank, holding horn,
as she, foreseeing Pasiphaë, bellowed my name.
I like a lady who will kneel before her lord, that he,
himself impatient of the yoke, might pizzle in her pasture.

Beneath bay leaves, with polished tusks, hieratic,
the head is carried in. The servant tilts the trencher
to his master who begins: "With eyes glowing, neck abristle,
chops foam flecked, this usurping swine wandered, uncastrated,
spoiling vines, uprooting garlands, until espying me
he raised his crown, imperious, bedecked;
and seeing such commodious array, I hired him."

The garish head turns upon its pivot and you, fearfully,
stare through the mask. I was instructed and I did the work
and now you'll pay for it. It's time to party!
Let's toss these coiffured locks in a dance.
Tradition says a shambles such as I must herald a god
but in my flesh each alienated part, combined, is Art.
Now, wait upon my swaying hips and shift your arse.

Coda

Chaos is the greater part of order. Truth employs procedures
to control. A gladsome oppressor, Love craves power. Listen,
a busy person cannot close their ears. The soul hears virtues
where the eye sees horror. One word shapes many worlds
whilst I, personifying productive power, embody its integrity.
Clean hands deceive a dirty mind. My maker made me
of the finest cuts and this is axiomatic—use me wisely.

ENGULFED

Across the park six girls ran
beneath enormous trees
as the heavens opened. Compromised,
like Ovid's nymphs, they danced
into a mist of spray.

It seemed to me that, unprepared,
they felt our mortal dilemma.
Each shrieking creature,
indistinct below the waist,
grew upon her silvered legs

such monstrous scales and fins
as ever lusty Triton fanned
in a green plunge.
Torn from history, these girls
have no sense of what is coming.

AMPHITRITE

The man caught by the tide, spewing water when they tipped his head,
intruded, passively, amongst the coloured balls and towels, the children
and the wives, of other people's holidays. But in being subject to a state
of erotic latency, as I was then, I stared at him, his vacancy, until
a lady, gentle and kind, insistent, introduced herself and turned me
from the water's edge. She said, "You don't really want to look at that…"

Pulling me along the beach, she showed me shells and stones within
still pools, whilst all the while I wanted to see that body. Her touch,
ambivalent, abides, yet years later I feel him there, still waiting.
With him, I'd wade into those overwhelming waves wanting
only to drown so she might find a life delivering the dead,
or, transforming everything, cast me on the loins of that moist god.

KILLING PHILOMEL

As one ordained by prophesy,
I stood on the lap of the Lady of Uruk.
She gazed with eyes of lapis lazuli,
through coils of hair, copper and gold,
and I touched her bosom as she spoke
to another behind me in the room.

Once I knew forgetfulness by heart,
and what it's meant to regulate,
but now, iconoclastic, I participate
in my past and, pushing back
through retrospective acts, annihilate
traditions others once cherished.

Every leaf on a Norfolk tree was royal.
We were loyal to an old magic, I knew that.
It didn't need to be said that in autumn,
becoming fiery, those leaves fell.
Later, furred with frost, they discharged
brightness rooted in the past, to honour us.

As might a lady stolen from a *Breton lai*,
alone, enchambered, summoning one lost,
see her own death approaching, so I,
gazing from a window at fieldfare and redwing,
absorbed in winter's bleak tillage,
hear strange calls unsettling the land.

I dreamed the world was a living tapestry.
In shades of gold, my hawk, killing Philomel,
placed the carcass in my hand.
Her silence entered mine.
With no voice of my own, I woke
to pipe the airs of that chaste throstle.

And lately the tendency has been for Art to enable repression.
Through Art sensibility and conscience are negated.
Despite the fawning, this renders makers respectable.
Und frische Nahrung, neues Blut saug ich aus freier Welt.
Pretending artistry may ransom debts but anyone can falsify,
forget, evade obscured relations otherwise hard to embody.
So, why the censorship? Is it to cover shame?

When Art replaces Nature as an image of the primal state
it is shown with Nature's virtues like a puppet on its knee.
Thus the lovely Artist, ventriloquising Nature,
hears itself in everything it sees. Redeemed as producer,
means of production and product, the Artist, self consuming,
is a kind of Ponzi scheme. Filled with narcissistic awe,
this creature swindles Nature of the law to get its justness.

GROTESQUERIES

Two heads cupped by leaves,
each gagging on a fruited stalk;
a gargoyle, upside down,
disgorging ornamental folds;
rain blown between trees which,
dipping and twisting, map
the chaos inside of me
upon which memory depends.
Grotesques bring back
the instant of the Fall.

Though *Some of them be treue*
of love, such songs as these
the body sings *Beneth the gerdell*,
for there one's figure divides.
Formless, by filth compelled,
and crude, the lower ranks equal
inferior parts, the arse, etc.,
the legs and feet.
Grotesques bring back
the instant of the Fall.

I have in my mind a warrior,
he was carved by a Norfolk man;
with sword and buckler, rapt,
spouting a flourish,
he witnesses epiphany.
It comes from his flesh.
His nature is revealed.
It hangs from the scouring.
Grotesques bring back
the instant of the Fall.

STURMDROSSEL

Some fragments

1.

Amongst ruins, as I sheltered from a storm,
a throstle recounted this poem which, it said,
was sung here "when the walls were strong."

2.

The citadel, falling, fulfils a prophecy
endorsed by mythic kings, Ybor and Agio,
and at this sign the implacable dead have risen.

3.

In funerary armour, gold masked, the king stood
with long dead Iope at his side, her diadem flaring.
This is how the minstrel described them.

4.

The hand that stilled my pen seeks to erase
what we, through warfare, conquering, achieved.
Armed, they take the place of those who fled.

5.

I told you dark was light and you believed.
Hearing that lowness was height, you kneeled.
When you did my bidding the dead were wrathful.

6.

The hand that stopped my mouth cannot silence
this incantation, for the storm-cock grips the bough
and shouts for joy though the tempest rages.

7.

Thunderously, gods long scorned lament.
Roots tear and branches fall when they howl.
Undaunted by my doom, I annunciate apocalypse.

SHANTY

He was off the Gulf of Corryvreckan,
trapped beneath the sea. The seer saw
Myrddin Emrys rotating in a whirlpool,
split from himself, gone turning, turning
in a mass of cobalt seagreen bubbles.
As inhibitions hold the self constrained,
I had been for a long time lost, my self
bound by an unknown potentiality within
the awkward presence I could never own,
the absence that defined me
as other than I might have been.

I climbed on rocks, fumbled hooks through
lugworm, lobbed tackle where the heave died,
lured pollock and bream, pulled clots of wrack
and kelp through foam and then the rod
knocked in my hand and I saw it, head
clear, as I stretched forward. I gaped at
monstrous lips when, probing its guts,
turning the key, personified, it apprehended me.

Ever since, in moments of possession,
when picturing what I will shortly have,
I face the facts of my true nature and,
as I acknowledge them, re-enact, stunned,
what was still in my hand—fast within
it hides, and nothing escapes
those black, unblinking eyes—
I feel the weight of it.

Coda
Were I, also, steadfast and vigilant, I'd never
have been caught by the bucking and writhing;
instead, in a flash, tilting the scales, I'd see
myself within that incomprehensible blur
and know my own ecstatic fall. Surfacing,
in my element, I would rejoice at the empty hand
and what had passed away, beyond its grasp.

SIGIL

The lady surveys interlocking circles
inscribed about the font to fascinate
demons and the unrepentant dead
who, jealous of life, would otherwise possess
the innocence of babes.
They'd take them, unbaptised.

She holds her torch obliquely to the wall
and, concentrating, leans closer.
That face, lit from below,
grimacing, with tongue outthrust
and deep enshadowed eyes, makes a mask
I might more safely observe in a mirror.

Tracing subtle lines, she describes
how evil, consigned, circles endlessly within;
that time, held like this,
in a church, is truly monumental.
"There's another here," she says,
inscribing an arc, drawing me in.

SWEET ROSY MOUTH

Basilicas exalt the graves of saints
but I, looking at admirable lives,
see only imaginary splendours.
Moonlight implies but does not define
fading glories as the sun declines.

Monumental, inviolable, wide-eyed,
with gaze fixed in remote prepossession,
embodying knowledge, this monarch admits
deposed powers that speak through objects
they possess, and so she takes my hand.

As wolf falls upon hind, the king,
annointed, through his mode of knowing,
sees through her eyes. All that is bright recedes.
Abode becomes reliquary.
Bones survive rendered flesh.

The dead reside within gestures.
They speak through manners yet to form.
Dea lunae. When they rejoice,
my queen, splendid in an aureole of rays,
will lead me from the charnel house.

FLOODED

The woods and moors were flooded and, in the town, shops
and houses floated on cellars filled with effluent. Springs
and wells, the silted ditches, stagnant for decades, stirred,
and the dead, snagged amongst roots and cables, slipped free.
Sliding down sewers, subterranean tributaries and drains,
they entered the river. Accumulating upstream of the mill,
the pressure, building, forced them through the filthy screw
until, churning and heaving, they passed under the bridge.

Figures rising from the vortex. Faces emerging. Actaeon,
tipped from riotous rout. Hounds at full pelt. Arethusa,
Urania, Theriope. A stag twisting in the gyre, uprearing,
arching back into oblivion. And this, I thought, is it;
the force rushing through us is death; felt as ecstasy,
it pulls us from flesh into nothingness. Your body
in the water, slipping away. Entangled arms and legs. And then
we passed beneath the motorway and entered the land beyond.

Lethe summons illusions that obscure former glories
and tradition, once noble and indifferent, now demonised,
becomes this longing for histories less negated. Remembrance
invokes the image of what is still possible. Green-black,
the river deepens. I searched for the dead and,
before memory was lost in the moment, glimpsed
my own vitality in time. I touched your arm and you,
looking back, catching my eye, reached into the abyss.

Venerable liberties, one lost in recollection walks a line,
turning and returning, as if memory and forgetting were a path
between two parishes. At the next church, we observed how
water lay in little pools on stones laid flat or toppled, revealing
here the hand that holds a book and there a skull engraved.
All about us Cherubim, who came to drink, were petrified.
Mirrored in water. Blind eyes. Where truth is not confessed,
virtue, unable to accommodate, is rendered into likeness.

You started at a sudden flare of light, harsh trumpet blasts,
a fierce uplifting of rooks as the sun, setting, glared sidelong
at us, lifting the granite lid that we, and what we mean,
might be illumined and truths, miraculous, revealed.
Flooded meadows, catching the flash of revelation,
provided such deliverance as we, going along with how
things seemed—the molten gold across the liquid surface—
might prefer to privately receive or, keeping low, ignore.

Stepping up, I looked into the church and saw two men,
armed, keeping watch from the other side. Witnessed within,
resplendent, these sentinels, each in his embrasure,
formidable, gazed on one who would become iridescent,
within the vision, like them. *And thence the light fades.*
They bar the way. Later, walking back along the lane,
we climbed the verge when vehicles passed, seeing trees
raise their arms in horror as cars sped by beneath them.

ACTAEON

You had black haired Melanchaetes
at your back, the killer,
Theridamas, by your side,
but you fell beneath my gaze.

Glanced by a deadly dart
cast by Cupid—it was
fired through the eye,
from behind a mask

not unlike your own—
I see you in the moment
when flesh becomes bone.
At your alarm, I tremble;

taking strength from your courage,
I participate; quickened
when you hurry, I flee
with you, racing the clouds.

What brightens dawn brilliance but the radiance of Christ?
Shielding their eyes, men stood back as, timbers warping,
fire levered strake from keel. Hull and cabin, blistering black,
collapsed; the heart-space of the hold that kept them strong,
burning, blurs their vision. Long before the boat was scrapped,
mother called me down to hear invocations, faint inside
pulsating static, Romulus to Remus. "That one's your dad,"
she said, tuning into swirling waves at his dark profanities.

The black dog, padding through shallows, scenting the tide,
arrives at dusk, opposite the quay, on the dark of the marsh
and looks in as one who watches shared intimacies
through an uncurtained window. The boat, brightly lit,
gives up its hoard of silvered black and slate blue fishes
and those sorting them, hauling the net, shifting crates,
shout and curse through the crackle and hiss that shields
their world from what darkness, closing in, reveals of his.

Forced by steep seas to return, held at the neap tide bar,
troubled, they see shore lights dimmed. Hearing the gale
testing doors, drawing curtains, a mother looks in
on one who, restless in sleep, heaves an image:
she sees bells shifting in the tower. All at once
the lifeboat launches a flare. Words whipped by squall
leave men speechless; the soul, dragged behind its shroud,
fast vanishing, illumines only black primordial waves.

Listen, I was at your heels from early on. I knew your lament
was my fate and you liked this familiar breathing at your back.
Think of me as memory, inheritance or tradition. Betrayal.
The family curse. I am your blood and here is my pedigree:
kicked and beaten, I was tied in a yard and starved;
leaping a fence, I was the yelping blur in which you hid
your misery. Shocked by my entrails, you looked away
as I ran to you, hopeful and afraid, eager with my load.

I sat with Shuck on a shingle bank. We tracked a child across
the freezing beach. Tongue lolling, I ran with the fiend.
The boy hurried into the wind, his eyes stung by salt and sand.
How it must hurt, I thought, to go into the gale and cry so.
With horror close by, I splashed through a pool. Turning his back,
the boy saw through grit and tears how forms break
at the edge of bleary distance, as we, still seeking oblivion
or shelter in the woods, left him to the void and bounded on.

When you raised your gun and, aiming, paused, I pre-empted
the detonation. Briefly, the world before the barrel warped;
the target folding in mid-flight, killed or wounded, fell.
I saw how it would be, the dogs, blameless and bold, leaping
tussock and bramble, leaning on each other as they ran.
Redeemed by death's brilliance, we suffered the pheasant
taking flight, calling, as I knew it would—the heart, stilled,
limp hood on golden feathers fading—the bloodied beak.

As the changeling in the cot laments the child, so the basilica,
raised from ruins long abandoned, commemorates apocalypse.
Fursa built at Burgh. Felix founded Dommoc in a fort left empty
by warlords who, fearing vengeance via offspring, would not lay
a wife on haunted ground. Where enemies chanted "Victory"
and then, defeated, died, the cuckoo celebrates its new allegiance.
Christ's men feared no demons, saw the life-giving Word
activate a pre-existing state and, spreading quickly, fill the land.

When old themes fail the battle rages in epic fragments.
Now Virtue's vast treasure burns before our eyes. Those loyal
look back to the stronghold where songs summoned gods
to their customary vengeance. Glasses gleamed. Exhaling,
she flicked ash whilst the old man laughed; each looked
to the other. Nigger and Paddy beneath the table, crowned
with burr and thistle-down, jerking and twitching at the kill;
warm plumage seeping, such joy as this we will never know.

The afterlife of the last lost age lingers. Embers flare. The fire
settling in the grate recalls bygone fires. Dog stench steaming,
a damp sack of chestnuts; amulets deployed about the hearth.
In the morning, knots of newspaper, the grid of kindling,
half laid, scenting the room, signals a new day.
I know it still and hear what was once inspiring
from one who, briefly lucid, remembers. Future and past
in one root, from one tongue springs the present like a flame.

THE KILL

In your room, holding the cartridge, you imagined flames
packed like petals in a bud, poppy red. Uncrimped, the hull
revealed, instead, only seeds. Having tasted saltpetre and sulphur,
ingested chemistry, mimed stock, action and barrel, linked
vital spark in hunter, gun and quarry, I saw combustion
through the engine of the hunt. This is what the kill entails:
the bird or animal, solemnly lifted, like one mourned,
hung, gutted, becomes the cavity my own ribs cradle.

Creeping out, first thing, I saw rows of pheasants, braced
for the butchers; the back garden, morbidly displaced.
Neither sensed nor seen by what went over my head,
motionless, I watched geese that caught the light at altitude.
Walking close behind, around field edge and marsh,
I came to know when to follow and when to be transfixed.
Be aware. You intrude. Unwelcome here. Keep low. Blend in.
Then make your move and picture yourself in the startled eye.

GRANDEUR

I sing this lament to mark the way that they might come back.
Although there seems to be no chance of restoration, this country
in being lost is known directly, not through the melancholy remnants
of the past, nor through songs and evocations, but in these last days,
where borders, buckled by storms, dissolve in shades that come
to let us know that whilst we persist, what we had is lost.

Guarded on the seaward side by an earthen bank, the steadings
and the fields. A cold blue lid containing the day within which
we picked potatoes into the dusk, insignificant figures working
the flat expanse. To show the force of images: my lord on the
threshold with a torch as I returned for the issue of a coin, for
products, institutions, rights; for liberties, once emblematic of the
state, as yet uncompromised; his light upon my face as I walked.

Just back from the colonies, they found a country in ruins,
imperial ports desolate, cities derelict. Bewildered warriors lament
force retreating into the past. The last of the speculators have
said their farewells and various pretenders, taking what they could,
have gone. When God has departed and the church is left,
the past, gold-bright, gleaming in splendour, becomes a living
thing once more and the presences referred to, which had
previously informed that continuity, are present again.

In the reception centre refugees sign for wealth, indicate permits,
recount lost hoards, plunder. They say they seek fixed benefits,
bonuses, a house not too far from the underworld. The speculator,
recounting his vision, mentioned risks internalised, a path down
into a deep unstable trough; the occult seer saw volatility, hedged
futures, lost holdings, the darkness engulfing Cornwall and Gaul.
We watched traffic slow to a halt. Money faltered. A false coinage
is no true reminder, the image hangs loose on its hinges.

In Saxon genealogies the father and son were paired. The latter
an echo of the former. Hroðmund and Hryp. Cerdic and Cynric.
The son no more than a counterpart, "to authenticate by repetition."
Shadowy in fact, that unknown figure, his features blurred by an act
of turning. The child occluded. Forced by the father to pursue
that fate he fought against, saw friends die for; afterwards he sought
his mother, finding then how his being might be erased by hers.

We saw, near Ipswich, the beaked frigate leaning on the barge
from which Edmund—descended from Erpenwald, descended
from Caesar and Woden—in stately progress surveyed the coast
of his kingdom, going from the Wash to Orford Ness, past
the rusted tankers, seeing the tips of mounds at Sutton Hoo.
Losing what they'd known and looking for the core of it, they
went out through Stratford, on to Romford and beyond, with each
migration staged as a pageant lost within the metaphor it raised.

They set to work building fires in the field maple, recreating scenes
from autumn, atmospheres. They watched you run outside to play
in a mythic space contrived of lights within which Yule could still
raise his cup of mead regardless and the congregation, although
dwindling, still sing. They promised ruddy fruits, the kingdom
on earth as it was before, renewed by their more vigorous belief,
the *folces cwen* Diana rising triumphant from the ruin of the car.

On the bus to Thetford, a baby with encephalitis bounces on its
mother's lap, hopefully attempting to engage with those who,
preferring to look away, glance out at fields and farmsteads passing by.
For this darkness, a boar upon the ritual helm. It peered out of the ark.
Outside Lackford, an imposing earthwork where, upon waking,
I felt that my head had grown vast; a great tumour on the earth;
a puffball placed upon a grave into which youths, for Hallowe'en,
had carved eyes and a mouth; I see how it regards me in the gloom,
the force of its smile coinciding with a sunburst in the world outside.

Ilford, Romford, Brentwood. Argent a cross gules;
banners, royal badges. The ruins bypassed in antiquity.
He looked silver in the fog, my *schucke* of the little fort;
hearth post, the defences restored, an English queen enthroned
once more; along the A12, as per US bases
in the war, at intervals, one every eight miles.

To arbitrate dissonance, that other Godric gone behind the shield wall;
now, behold, where levies formed up in the discrepancy between
the rich men's sons who ran away and their heroic stand; a poem
to distinguish a nation. Between fact and legend, *Byrhtnoð mapelode,*
bord hafenode | Byrhtnoth made a speech within which we contend.
Coding difference and similarity, the poem extends automatic systems
in the brain; so what might be reconciled between those who survived,
and what they lost, and the traitors who did not look back to those days
when everything, located in the future, shone, and the foe as yet had
left unoccupied unguarded ground where I had been and I belong?

Mars as ever Mars must be; beyond shame, the warrior silent for years,
unresolved, his thoughts given as goods through passions imposed—
for the losses of gay kynges heaped, dishonoured pale, modern politics
within which poets variously comply, their material adjusted to please;
and all for a thumbs up on Facebook! The gentleman raised his shield
at Massacres Direct and signed up for the full experience as I, dithering,
gave up my rights for there are many Hamlets in this village and each
prince, compromised, must these long winters pass the gelding in the field.

When I looked from the train, cranes rising from inside the stadium
appeared to hold it above the world; an object lifted from within.
The world writ small in narrative, Olympian or Imperial, is suspended
within the one void that we, unequally, all share. And so her Majesty,
impersonating the Crown, enacts her namesake on the royal barge.
In white with a silver breastplate, her helmet on a cushion born
by a page, she rides her grey gelding through scenes allegorical,
o'erpicturing foreign tyranny with an image lifted from *The Faerie Queene*.
Chased wives might turn, a weapon in their hand, fierce where we
see fancy outwork nature, to hold them back, that would in error fall.

In days of old they said she first ascended, in skirts of lead, with
grey crystals of lead formate folded and corroded about her throat.
Head tilted. "And her lips were dusted with white powder."
The widow of the conquered king rising on unsteady feet to haul her
body back into the brilliance of my words; a pool of light
through which she comes to me for the ordeal of the long walk
back toward the grave; the dead cow suckling its calf; the spectre,
sensed as formidable, appalled by what we have done to the past.

Playing at the edge of a creek, her legs neatly stockinged in
black mud, her face caked in that muck, the others like tar babies,
and this couture a parody of my glamours: I heard them arguing
outside, the animals in the compound releasing their odours,
and I touched myself and they called her from the water's edge
saying look at the state of you and all the time within
her hand the slate blue-black mussel clamped shut.

When the police arrived I merged with the bushes and watched
the archaic constable who, upon climbing from his car, grew larger
as if some libidinous god had entered him. He embodied the fertility
figured in his sex as he laboured up the path and I, the shadow
of Dame Nature, dark within the wood, remarked how bright Hector
beneath Ilium had never looked so good. I saw you pause to scratch
your head, flat cap in hand. The conscious I standing close to the Id
and looking vulnerable. Father, where forces without names
form paths, authority—knowing only victims and witnesses
as sources—itself is modified by what it seeks to name and seize.

Elmham: The material and mechanical forces of the poem
form in structures at once felt and then revealed,
these might translate via mathematics into some other form.
The past, illuminated in manuscripts denoting powers
the mighty once endorsed, was forced by beauty through the
forms of things; in those days it worked at such intensity
that men mutated, uttered leaves from their mouths,
and women became trees—thus were all things given meaning.

Concerning stately splendours lost, deficit and debt, romances
retrieved from false accounts, figures glossed that seemed reliable
once, outstanding, I sense glory pending payment of account.
Enduring gold, goldleaf on frames, landscapes in which men,
as Midas to the world, in pasture-light, magnificent, are golden.
Beneath goatskins, tragic clowns, redeemed. From what was deep
and hidden once now fulsome grow soft unfurling leaves.

In yielding to my form I saw how the father had prepared for
my ascent into matters since identified with him, his mode
of standing. In *Beowulf* the lady extends the power of her lord.
Pater Europæ, I reached through his gesture, the morning adding
lustre to that movement, the clamour of armour giving form to what
hides within; and Mars alighting upon the mere stood blushing
before my love, the small points of his rays tipped with vermilion.

In Elmet or Lindsey, where time adorns bankrupt kings,
the warriors who kept their lords for the worship
and gifts they gave lie crouched beyond the oppidum,
on hilltop and ridge, with their beakers and their pins.
Leaving the mouth, a tendril curls on the lip; rooted in
what life once lacked my flesh holds the certainty of the depth
and efficacy that streamed, at evening, through the open window.

There is no history of truth. Lies, in time, accumulate. Treason
overthrows no godly monarch. Generous comes from noble birth.
Trusty means related. After time, taking the churchyard home,
clamorous, these lads, *Hlude wæran hy, la, hlude, ða hy ofer*
þone hlæw ridan where one knocks down a pot of flowers.
Maiden reprobate, shield yourself beneath the linden tree.
Erce. Erce. Eorþan modor remote states legislate against kith
and kin and no plausible minstrel infers what this might mean.

Displacing some pre-Indo-European goddess of abundance,
a container ship proceeds with the import and pomp of a queen.
Mater materia, tugged from an abyss, power made manifest,
resplendent in fable, once pacifying monsters with archaic force,
your peoples, the ancient seafarers, have been replaced.
There is not one undeniable fact upon which history turns.
Fixed between gantries, the ship dominates dusk on the river.

Got me up at 4 a.m. to look through the Velux. Dog Star
magnified by jaundiced murk over the A12, pulsating
evil ore alight; waxing gibbous moon; Orion astride
derelict sheds commanding fume and smoke, foretelling
landscapes blotted, states falling, enemies abroad,
their inspired utterance lauding starry revelations.

Goes back to bed. Can't sleep. Listens to her breathing. Feels
horns forming on his head. Thinks savage thoughts. Sleeps.
Dreams his stag night in St Osyth. Trots to The White Hart.
Meets SS Hubert, Eustachius, Aidan, Julian Hospitaller and Felix
who ensure he acts the part omitted from the play outlined
in the *Grotte des Trois-Frères*. As it happens, during the pursuit,
he sees how the soul of the quarry is stripped of its radiance
as skin is pulled from an animal killed in the depths of a forest.

Listen! A wind disturbs the trees. They signal the presence
of animating forces no-one can see. Come, sister, let us sit
by the window and embroider new epic ages. Tell me what appears
when the point, rending fabric, rises and I'll bring a look
of triumph to the face of Isabella of Castille. Some unseen other
threads my eye. It draws dignity from flesh at one with history.
With steady hand and firm grip I'll place russet light behind her.

Upcycled tat once won in mythic wastes, now preloved.
Reconditioned themes in tarnished sagas glossed,
with new forms uncoiling at the margins. Sold as pillage,
must-have legendary queens in shabby chic. They enter
on his word—Modthryth flanked by Wealhþēow and Hygd—
shocked virtue enshadowed by the frame, gaunt faces
catching light as they turn and all the hall applauds.

As once a lord protected his retinue, so you kept me safe
from knowledge of olden times; memories, latent reminders.
In photos mother and father in shadow as gods since slighted
assembled behind them: Woden and Frige, hallowed and proud,
holding the infant. *Keep your eye on him*. Went back after
many years. Remembered slack water, a boat tugging
at its rope. As before, ebb tides draw unutterable burdens.

Beauty will not force a way through me, but I can still
describe its absences, knowing loveliness by the crude
lines of my face and tenderness by my rough hand.
I shelter in this place, graven in black stone, my hand
always close to my mouth; my dog captured in
its turning to a movement quite close by. Loyal and true,
he turns his head to snarl at those who chance to look
where I lie, long since forgotten, in this vast futurity.

Notes

Page 12   *Epigram*

> Here are maidens
> in a circle;
> they'd like to be without a lover
> all the summer through.

The original is in Middle High German. It is poem 129a in the 1847 Johann Andreas Schmeller collected edition of *Carmina Burana* (Songs from Benediktbeuern). The translation above is from the programme for a production of Carl Orff's 1935 cantata, *Carmina Burana* (Royal Philharmonic Orchestra, Royal Festival Hall, May 1986). *Translation © 1937 Schott Music International, copyright renewed.*

Page 15   *"As I sat reading quaint old English verse…"*

The trap was set between pages 260 and 261 of *The Poems of the Pearl Manuscript – Pearl, Cleanness, Patience, Sir Gawain and the Green Knight* (Exeter: University of Exeter Press 2002), edited by Malcolm Andrew and Ronald Waldron. I was drawn into an account of the bringing to bay of a boar, "borelych and brode, bor alþer-grattest" (line 1441). Once slain, with my head on a pole, I was paraded through a similar scene in John Audelay's 'Three Dead Kings'. See *Poems and Carols* (Oxford: Bodleian Library MS Douce 302), edited by Susanna Greer Fein: http://d.lib.rochester.edu/teams/text/fein-audelay-poems-and-carols-meditative-close (Accessed 5/7/20).

In my poem the beast, shifting its shape, becomes a hind. In combining man, hind and wild boar, I create a composite, epicene creature, made of torn flesh, lifted offal, butchered meat. This, it seems, is my emblem.

Page 17   *"As if cut from paper…"*

This image is from Sir Gawain and the Green Knight, line 802. "Þhat pared out of papure purely hit semed."

See page 238 of *The Poems of the Pearl Manuscript* (details above). As the footnote explains, "The castle is compared to the paper cut-outs which some-times decorated food brought to table in 14th c. banquets. Chaucer's parson speaks of *pride of the table … in … swich manere bake-metes and disshmetes, brennynge of wilde fir and peynted and castelled with papir*."

Likewise, the deep double ditch, complete with tarrying horsemen, first flickered into view on page 237, line 786, and in footnote 785f, of the same book.

Page 21   *"Belinda, sportive play'd…"*

Once trafficked by Alexander Pope, I found Belinda and Eloisa working a sonnet by William Sotheby (1757–1833), 'Written at Bevis Mount, 1782': "Oft at his call, these sunny glades among / Thy guardian Sylphs, Belinda, sportive play'd, / And Eloisa sigh'd in yon sequester'd shade." *They can still be found at weekends plying their trade on Empress Road.* Pope had them in 'The Rape of the Lock' and 'Eloisa to Abelard'. Belinda was known to Martial. Eloisa sigh'd for obvious reasons.

Page 22   *The Trusty Servant*

"**Trusty Servant, Trusty Sweater, Trusty Pig** picture symbolising the virtues of a perfect College servant, affixed to the west wall of the room called Ante-kitchen (1838), Buttery (1892), Trusty Sweater's Hole (1917)…

This emblem first appears in sixteenth-century costume in the manuscript of 'De Collegiata Schola [Wicchamica]'. The picture has been several times repainted, and in 1778 it was altered to eighteenth-century costume in honour of George III's visit. Aubrey records that the pleasant Latin elegaics accompanying the picture were composed by a brilliant College boy named John Hoskins (1566–1638). The English verse translation and the original picture itself may have been done by him while still in College (c. 1580)."

Winchester Notions – The English Dialect of Winchester College, Charles Stevens (The Athlone Press, 1998).

The epigram is from the 'Boar's Head Carol' published in *Middle English Lyrics*, Eds. Maxwell S. Luria and Richard L. Hoffman (Norton Critical Editions 1974), see page 139. *Servitur cum sinapio*. It is served with mustard.

Page 30   *"Und frische Nahrung…"*

The quotation is from Johann Wolfgang Von Goethe's 'Auf dem See' (On the Lake). Here is the complete sentence: "Und frische Nahrung, neues Blut / Saug ich aus freier Welt; / Wie ist Natur so hold und gut, / Die mich am Busen hält!" (And I suck fresh nourishment, new blood, out of untrammelled nature: how gracious and generous is Nature, who holds me to her bosom!). *Blut ist Milch.* See: *The Penguin Book of German Verse,* Introduced and Edited by Leonard Forster (Penguin Books, 1967) for both the poem and translation used here.

Page 31   *"Some of them be treue of love / Beneth the gerdell . . ."*

> Some of them be treue of love
> Beneth the gerdell, but nat above,
> And in a hode aboue can chove…

From 'Women', a lyric appended to *The Wright's Chaste Wife - A Merry Tale* (c. 1462), by Adam of Cobsam.

http://www.luminarium.org/medlit/medlyric/women.php
(Accessed 05/07/20).

Page 59   *"There is no history of Truth."*

The old English is from Foys, Martin, *et al.*, eds. *Old English Poetry in Facsimile*, Center for the History of Print and Digital Culture, University of Wisconsin-Madison. https://uw.digitalmappa.org/58 (Accessed 18/02/21). The quotes are from 'For a Sudden Stitch' and 'For Unfruitful Land'.

Hlude wæran hy, la, hlude,   ða hy ofer þone hlæw ridan
They were loud, lo, loud, those who were riding over the mounds
Erce, Erce, Erce,   eorþan modor
Yrce, Yrce, Yrce, mother of the earth,

Note: these translations are from Aaron K. Hostetter's *Old English Poetry Project*. https://oldenglishpoetry.camden.rutgers.edu (Accessed 18/02/21)

Erce: Attested in the 11th-century *Æcerbot* ("field-remedy") charm. The triple invocation *erce, erce, erce* is compared to the Latin *sanctus, sanctus, sanctus*, and interpreted as derived from a vocative form of *eorcnan* "true, genuine; holy", or a proper name *Erce*, from an earlier *Eorce* for a fertility goddess addressed as "mother of earth".

See: "erce" – *WordSense Online Dictionary*. https://www.wordsense.eu/erce (Accessed 18/02/21)

9 781848 618442